Bryn Mawr Latin Commentaries

Concilium
Romarici Montis

Paul Pascal

Thomas Library
Bryn Mawr College
Bryn Mawr, Pennsylvania

Copyright ©1993 by **Bryn Mawr Commentaries**

Manufactured in the United States of America
ISBN 0-929524-77-2
Printed and distributed by
Bryn Mawr Commentaries
Thomas Library
Bryn Mawr College
101 North Merion Avenue
Bryn Mawr, PA 19010-2899

Introduction

The *Concilium Romarici Montis* is an account in Latin verse of a mock church council said to have been held at Remiremont (*Romarici Mons*), not far from Nancy and Strasbourg in eastern France. The Council was convened by the nuns of the royal abbey of Remiremont, a religious community whose members were recruited from the nobility. The abbey had already been in existence for about five hundred years when the poem was composed in the twelfth century.

The subject of the Council is Love; accordingly the opening ceremonies include a reading from Ovid's *Ars Amatoria*. A Lady Cardinal (*Cardinalis Domina*), decked in spring flowers, presides over the deliberations, which quickly turn into a formal debate on the relative merits of the knight (*miles*) and the clerk (*clericus*) as lovers. Representatives of the two factions of ladies extol their candidates and disparage the opposition (at quite unequal length; the women who favor the *clerici* are given much more than their fair share of time). Finally a vote is taken, and the *Cardinalis Domina* declares the unsurprising result: henceforth only clerks are to be eligible as lovers for the ladies of Remiremont. Whoever fails to honor this decision is solemnly excommunicated.

Several of the women who participate in the Council are named in the poem, resulting in a heightened appearance of reality. The keeper of the gate is *Sibilia* (line 19), whose name suggests pagan associations with Apollo. *Eva de Danubrio* (line 29; *Deneuvre* in modern French) is the reader of the "Gospel" of Ovid. Two girls named *Elizabet* (line 33) sing hymns of love to inaugurate the Council. Several more are named only in subheads that are provided in the manuscripts of the poem: before line 61, *Elizabet de Granges* and before line 67, *Elizabet de Falcon* (these two being perhaps identical with the singers); before lines 94, 100, 115, and 121, *Agnes*, *Berta*, *Elizabet Popona*, and *Adeleyt*. Most of these names can be at least tentatively identified with those of real women who were members of the religious community of Remiremont, according to surviving documents of the period.[1]

The poem is, of course, anonymous. Most likely it is by a local clerk, perhaps one from Toul (see lines 10-15); but the possibility should not be excluded that it was written by one (or more?) of the women of Remiremont. It would be useful to know the precise date of the poem in order to place it accurately in the history of the theme of courtly love. Paleographical and stylistic evidence, and such evidence as that of the proper names, all suggest a date in approximately the middle of the twelfth century.

The motif of a formal debate is a common one in literature, occurring as early as Greek tragedy and in the *agon* of Aristophanic comedy. In the medieval period we find poetic debates, both serious and satirical, between spring and summer, the violet and the rose, wool and linen, wine and water, body and soul, and many others. The particular theme of the debate in the *Concilium Romarici Montis*, the merits of various types of men as lovers, has roots that can plausibly be traced as far back as the legends of the Trojan War. In classical Latin literature, a close analogy to the relative merits of "knight" and "clerk" as lover can be found in Ovid, *Amores* III.8. The *Altercatio Phyllidis et Florae*, an elegant long Latin poem in the Goliardic meter nearly contemporary with the *Concilium Romarici Montis*, deals with the same theme.[2]

Until the *Cardinalis Domina* begins her final impassioned speech of excommunication (line 205), the *Concilium Romarici Montis* is organized into three-line stanzas. The lines in each stanza are linked not by rhyme, but as clear sense-units; so clear that where the pattern seems to fail, emendation is almost certainly called for.[3] The rhythm is trochaic and is based on word accent.

---

[1] The most thorough study of the names of these women is in Lee (see Bibliography below), pp. 69 ff. The *Cardinalis Domina* is the only individual not given a name in the manuscripts of the poem; her dress and behavior support the view that she is intended as a symbolic figure. At one point, in fact, she refers to herself as an outsider (l. 53).

[2] The *Altercatio Phyllidis et Florae* is one of the *Carmina Burana* (Number 92). Excerpts of it are included in F. J. E. Raby's *Secular Latin Poetry* (2:191 ff.), and in the same author's *Oxford Book of Medieval Latin Verse*, pp. 312 ff.

[3] See below, p. 5.

There are many displacements of the trochaic beat. The lines contain fourteen syllables and break in the middle so that every half-line contains three and a half trochees. Each line almost without exception constitutes a grammatical unit in itself, with no interlocking or carryover between lines.[4] In fact, there is not often any grammatical carryover even between half-lines. A two-syllable internal rhyme marks the middle and end of each line.[5]

The *Concilium Romarici Montis* is preserved for us in two manuscripts, both currently in libraries located near where the events of the poem are supposed to have taken place. The earlier manuscript is in Trier.[6] It appears to have been written about the middle of the twelfth century, although the precise dating is still a matter of discussion. The other manuscript was originally from Rommersdorf, and is now preserved in Koblenz.[7] The consensus of paleographers is that it was written in the thirteenth century. There is no indication of stanza division in T, while R is laid out not as verse, but as prose paragraphs. The manuscripts appear to be independent of each other, as each has corruptions and omissions peculiar to itself. R omits lines 131-62 altogether; also lines 27-28, 67-69,

---

[4]The only real exceptions are at lines 7-8 and 109-10, both times involving the carryover of the word *Amoris*. The word then is intended to come as something of a surprise, after a brief pause.

[5]Rhyming in Latin, largely because of the inflectional endings, is such an easy effect that it takes special effort to avoid it. Good classical stylists regarded such patterns as *multorum virorum bonorum* with disdain. Not so in the case of many medieval Latin poets, even where the most commonplace endings were concerned. It is instructive to observe how many of the lines of the *Concilium Romarici Montis* have such banal rhymes as *-ibus*, *-imus*, or *-ia*. (Between lines 109 and 115, for example, this last rhyme occurs four times.) The poet does avoid repeating the same rhyme in two consecutive lines within the same stanza. This circumstance adds some support to the placement of line 44 in its new position there; see below, page 5. About the best that can be said for the rhymes in the *Concilium Romarici Montis* is that most of them are at least accurate. Lines 33, 218, and 241 are mildly aberrant; only line 148 is so much so as to be actually somewhat suspect. See Commentary on line 148.

[6]Stadtbibliothek 1081, hereafter T.

[7]Landeshauptarchiv 162, 1401, hereafter R.

and 124-26, as well as parts of several others. Where the two manuscripts differ, sometimes one and sometimes the other appears to preserve the correct text. When all other means of choosing between variant readings fail, as a last resort the reading of T, the earlier and more complete manuscript, is adopted into the present text. In punctuation and spelling, the principal criteria for this edition have been clarity and the convenience of the student. The punctuation of the manuscripts has been ignored; all punctuation has been provided by the editor. Such spellings in the manuscripts as *moncium* and *senciunt* for *montium* and *sentiunt*, and *-e* for *-ae* or *-oe*, have been consistently standardized to the classical form. Variant readings and emendations are not discussed in the Commentary except in a few particularly interesting cases. Accordingly, students should remain aware that for spelling and for most textual matters they must turn to critical editions.[8]

A few textual matters call for brief discussion here. The title, IDUS APRILIS HABITUM EST CONCILIUM HOC IN MONTE ROMARICI, appears only in T; R gives no title. The poem in T ends with a single line, *Ad confirmationem omnes dicimus Amen*, spoken by the women in unison to ratify the anathemas of the *Cardinalis Domina*. The line is more or less in the trochaic meter of the rest of the poem; rather exceptionally it displays imperfect rhyme (see footnote 4 above). It is not included in R, which ends with a single quantitative dactylic hexameter, at variance with the accentual trochaic meter of the body of the poem: MILITIBUS VICTIS, CESSIT VICTORIA CLERO. It may be that either, both, or neither of these two concluding lines belong to the original poem.

The subheads that appear sporadically in the body of the text in the manuscripts indicate a change of speaker, or in a few cases serve to set off sections of one speech.[9] Before line 215, where T has *Excommunicatio Rebellarum*, R has simply *Excommunicatio*.[10] I have inserted subheads or indications of subheads which are in neither manuscript, but where changes of speaker must occur,

---

[8] For this purpose, Lee will be found the most useful.

[9] The subheads before lines 61 and 67 are present only in T, the ones before lines 94, 100, 103, 106, 109, 115, 121, 172, 178, 184, 199, 202, and 205 only in R.

[10] See **Commentary** on line 215.

before lines 49, 133, 154, and 157; also before the single concluding line in T. The most interesting textual question in the *Concilium Romarici Montis* has to do with the division of the poem into three-line stanzas. From its beginning to the concluding speech of the *Cardinalis Domina* (lines 1-204), this division can be detected clearly, despite the absence of stanza division in T and the prose layout of R. Every three-line group constitutes an independent sense unit, ending in a full stop. Individual speeches are in multiples of three lines. The very few apparent exceptions stand out in such a manner as to invite critical intervention. The pattern can be made perfectly regular by moving one line, and by assuming four lacunas totaling five lines. Previous editors have suggested various specific remedies to implement this. The line that is moved in the present edition (*convocavit singulas, magnas atque parvulas*) follows line 30 in the manuscripts, where it makes no sense. There is obviously something missing after line 43; moving the line in question to that position fills the gap appropriately and restores the three-line pattern at both points. The lacunas assumed here are marked as lines 16, 58, 97-98, and 189.

The *Concilium Romarici Montis* was forgotten for centuries until 1849 when it was first edited by Georg Waitz, who knew only the Trier manuscript. Wilhelm Meyer reedited the text in 1914 using both T and R. The most recent (1981) and most thorough study of the work, complete with an English translation and detailed critical apparatus, is by Reuben R. Lee.[11]

No one is likely to claim a place for the *Concilium Romarici Montis* as a masterpiece of Medieval Latin verse. It would be easy to compile from it a long list of grammatical and stylistic infelicities. Still it deserves to be read as an early example in Latin of a poem dealing with elements of the theme of courtly love, which becomes an important one in the vernacular literatures. It also has the special interest of giving prominence to the role of several outspoken medieval women. Finally, most readers will find it delightful

---

[11] For details of these works, see **Bibliography** below. Lee provides an excellent bibliography (pp. vii-xvii), complete to 1981. Substantial accounts of the *Concilium Romarici Montis* can be found in C. S. Lewis, *The Allegory of Love* (Oxford, 1938, reprinted 1967); F. J. E. Raby, *A History of Secular Latin Poetry in the Middle Ages* (Oxford, 1957); and Peter Dronke, *Medieval Latin and the Rise of European Love-Lyric* (Oxford, 1968).

and amusing, and at the same time tantalizing, as it presents a vivid satirical picture of some novel aspects of medieval life and thought.

Bibliography

Lee, Reuben R. "A New Edition of *The Council of Remiremont*." Unpublished dissertation, University of Connecticut (1981).

Meyer, Wilhelm. "Das Liebesconcil in Remiremont," *Göttinger Nachrichten* (1914): 1-19.

Waitz, Georg. "Das Liebesconcil," *Zeitschrift für deutsches Altertum* 7 (1849): 160-67; supplemented in the same journal, 21, n. f. 9 (1877): 65-68.

Warren, F. M. "The Council of Remiremont," *Modern Language Notes* 22 (1907): 137-140.

IDUS APRILIS HABITUM EST CONCILIUM HOC IN MONTE ROMARICI:

Veris in temporibus sub Aprilis Idibus
habuit concilium Romarici montium
puellaris contio montis in coenobio.
Tale non audivimus nec fuisse credimus
5   in terrarum spatio a mundi principio.
Tale numquam factum est sed neque futurum est.

In eo concilio de solo negotio
Amoris tractatum est, quod in nullo factum est;
sed de Evangelio nulla fuit mentio.
10   Nemo qui vir dicitur illuc intromittitur.
Quidam tamen aderant qui de longe venerant.
Non fuerunt laici sed honesti clerici.

Ianua Tullensibus aperitur omnibus
quorum ad solacium factum est concilium.
15   Hos honestos sentiunt, intus et suscipiunt.

< . . . . >
puellis amantibus. Illis solis omnibus
ianua dat aditum ceteris prohibitum.

Ianuae custodia fuit haec Sibilia
quae ab annis teneris miles facta Veneris
quicquid Amor iusserat non invita fecerat.

Veteranae dominae arcentur a limine
quibus omne gaudium solet esse taedium,
gaudium et cetera quae vult aetas tenera.

Intromissis omnibus virginum agminibus,
lecta sunt in medium, quasi Evangelium,
praecepta Ovidii, doctoris egregii.

Lectrix tam propitii fuit Evangelii
Eva de Danubrio, potens in officio
artis amatoriae, ut affirmant aliae.

Cantus modulamina et amoris carmina
cantaverunt pariter, satis et sonoriter
de multis non quaelibet, duae sed Elizabet.

Has duas non latuit quicquid Amor statuit.
Harum in notitia ars est amatoria;
sed ignorant opere quid vir sciat facere.

Post haec oblectamina Cardinalis Domina
adstitit in medio, indicto silentio,
vestita, ut decuit, veste qua refloruit.

Haec vestis, coloribus colorata pluribus,
gemmis fuit clarior, auro pretiosior,
mille Maii floribus hinc inde pendentibus.

Ipsa virgo regia, mundi flos et gloria,
convocavit singulas, magnas atque parvulas,
florens super omnia quasi Veris filia.

Haec talis in omnibus docta satis artibus,
habens et facundiam secundum scientiam,
postquam coetus siluit ora sic aperuit.

<CARDINALIS DOMINA>

      Vos quarum est gloria amor et lascivia
50   atque delectatio Aprilis cum Maio:
      notum vobis facimus, ad vos quare venimus.

      Amor, deus omnium quotquot sunt amantium,
      me misit vos visere et vitam inquirere.
      Sic Maius disposuit et Aprilis monuit.

55   Vos ergo benigniter et amicabiliter
      obtestor et moneo, sicut iure debeo:
      nulla vestrum sileat quae vos vita teneat.

      < . . . . >
      Si quid corrigendum est vel si cui parcendum est,
60   meum est corrigere, meum est et parcere.

ELIZABET DE GRANGES LOQUITUR:

      Nos ex quo potuimus Amori servivimus.
      Quicquid ipse voluit nobis non displicuit,
      et si quid negleximus, inscienter fecimus.

      Sic servando regulam nullam viri copulam
65   habendam eligimus sed neque cognovimus,
      nisi talis hominis qui sit nostri ordinis.

ELIZABET DE FALCON:

Clericorum gratiam, laudem et memoriam
nos semper amavimus et amare cupimus,
quorum amicitia nil tardat solacia.

70 Clericorum copula, haec est nostra regula,
nos habet et habuit et placet et placuit,
quos scimus affabiles, gratos et amabiles.

Inest curialitas clericis et probitas.
Non noverunt fallere neque maledicere.
75 Amandi peritiam habent et industriam.

Pulchra donant munera, bene servant foedera.
Si quid amant dulciter, non relinquunt leviter.
Pro his quos assumpsimus ceteros postponimus.

Vota stulta frangere non est nefas facere.
80 Nulla est damnatio sed neque transgressio,
si votum negligitur quod stulte promittitur.

Experto credendum est, cuï bene certum est,
certum est et cognitum quid sit amor militum,
quam sit detestabilis, quam miser et labilis.

85 Per insipientiam, eorum notitiam
in primis quaesivimus sed cito cessavimus,
dolus ut apparuit, in eis qui latuit.

Inde nos transtulimus ad hos quos notavimus,
quorum est dilectio omni carens vitio,
90 quorum amor utilis, firmus est et stabilis.

Quid dicemus amplius, nisi quod ulterius
nulla valet ratio a nostro solacio
clericos disiungere omni gratos opere?

AGNES:

      Puellis claustralibus vobis dico omnibus:
95   magna est abusio militum susceptio.
      Nefas est et vetitum et vobis illicitum.

      < . . . .
      . . . . >
      amplectendo clericum; sic recuso laicum.

BERTA:

100 Amor, deus omnium, iuventutis gaudium,
      clericos amplectitur et ab eis regitur.
      Tales ergo diligo, stultos quoque negligo.

OMNES ISTAE LOQUUNTUR:

      Tali vita vivimus, in qua permanebimus
      si vobis laudabilis videtur et utilis;
105 et si quid peccavimus, si vultis, cessabimus.

CARDINALIS DOMINA:

      Ipsis amatoribus circumspectis omnibus,
      utiles non adeo amatores video
      quam istos quos laudibus praefertis in omnibus.

MILITARES ETIAM LOQUUNTUR:

      Nos a pueritia semper in familia
110   Amoris permansimus et manere cupimus.
      Sed est nobis alia amandi sententia.

      Qui student militiae nobis sunt memoriae.
      Horum et militia placet et lascivia.
      Horum ad obsequium nostrum datur studium.

ELIZABET POPONA:

115   Audaces ad proelia sunt pro nostra gratia.
      Ut sibi nos habeant et ut nobis placeant,
      nulla timent aspera, nec mortem nec vulnera.

      Tales praeelegimus, tales nostros fecimus.
      Eorum prosperitas est nostra felicitas.
120   Eorum tristitia nostra turbat gaudia.

ADELEYT:

      Semper ex quo potui sectam illam tenui,
      et semper desidero, dum habere potero,
      servire militibus mihi servientibus.

      Tale vero studium magis quam psalterium,
125   talibus me iungere placet plus quam legere.
      Propter horum copulam parvi pendo regulam.

      Nostrum illis atrium est et erit pervium,
      et fontem et pascua quae habemus congrua
      equis exposuimus quos eorum novimus.

130 Tali vita vivere gaudemus summopere
quia nulla dulcior nullaque commodior
et quia sic novimus et sancte iuravimus.

<CHANGE OF SPEAKERS:>

Nos parum regnavimus, parum adhuc fecimus,
sed flores colligere, rosas primas carpere,
135 his tantum concessimus quos de clero novimus.

Haec nostra professio erit et intentio:
clericis ad libitum persolvere debitum,
quotquot oblectamina viro debet femina.

Idem proposuimus et voto firmavimus,
140 quicquid dicant aliae nobis adversariae.
Clericis nos dedimus nec eos mutabimus.

Clericorum probitas et eorum bonitas
semper quaerit studium ad amoris gaudium,
sed eorum gaudia tota ridet patria.

145 Laudant nos in omnibus rhythmis atque versibus.
Tales, iussu Veneris, diligo prae ceteris.
Dulcis amicitia clericis est gloria.

Quicquid dicant aliae, apti sunt in opere.
Clericus est habilis, dulcis et affabilis.
150 Hunc habendo socium, nolo maius gaudium.

Omne votum utile firmum sit et stabile.
Sed quod est illicitum habeatur irritum,
nam stulta promissio non est absque vitio.

<CARDINALIS DOMINA:>

155　　Vos quarum prudentia apta dat consilia,
　　　nunc illud attendite et bene discernite:
　　　amor quarum aptior, quarum est deterior?

<CHANGE OF SPEAKERS:>

　　　Militum notitia displicet et gratia,
　　　quibus inest levitas et stulta garrulitas.
　　　Gaudent maledicere, secretum detegere.

160　　Hoc ergo consilium damus et iudicium:
　　　ut cunctis odibiles sint et execrabiles
　　　quae se militaribus implicant amoribus.

　　　< . . . . >
　　　novi vitam omnium et mores amantium;
165　　novi qui sint mobiles et nobis inutiles.

　　　Nulla est felicitas sed neque fidelitas
　　　in amore militum, quod est multis cognitum.
　　　Hos vitandos ducimus et iure decernimus.

　　　Clericos diligere bonum est et sapere.
170　　Eorum dilectio magna delectatio.
　　　Hos tantum suscipite, ceteros postponite.

CARDINALIS DOMINA:

　　　Quia sic decernitis et iure consulitis
　　　nunc ego praecipio, eas in consortio
　　　nostrae non recipiant nisi satisfaciant.

175 Sed si paenituerint et se nobis dederint,
 detur absolutio et talis condicio,
 ne sic peccent amplius, quia nil deterius.

NOTA ALIUD DICTUM:

 Hoc mandamus etiam per obedientiam:
 nulla vestrum pluribus se det amatoribus.
180 Uni soli serviat et ille sufficiat.

 Hoc si qua neglexerit, banno nostro suberit.
 Non levis remissio fiet huic vitio.
 Levi paenitentia non purgantur talia.

ITEM ALIUD DICTUM

 Nunc demum praecipio, sed non sub silentio,
185 ne vos detis vilibus nec umquam militibus
 tactum vestri corporis, vel coxae vel femoris.

 Talibus solacium dare vel colloquium
 dolor nobis maximus est et pudor plurimus.
 < .... >

190 Militum solacia nobis sunt opprobria,
 quia cum non creditur fama turpis oritur,
 quorum ex infamia nostra perit gloria.

 Precor vos summopere clericos diligere,
 quorum sapientia disponuntur omnia,
195 totum quicquid agimus, vel cum nos desipimus.

 Causas nostras agere student atque regere
 quantum possunt; etiam per eorum gratiam
 nostra quaedam abdita numquam erunt cognita.

CARDINALIS DOMINA AD OMNES:

200   Si placent quae diximus, quae vobis suggerimus,
horum confirmatio sit vestra responsio.
Si cuï displiceat, haec nequaquam taceat.

OMNES RESPONDENT:

Omnis nostra contio sedens in concilio,
ut vestra prudentia dictat, laudat omnia.
Placet iunioribus, placet nobis omnibus.

ITEM CARDINALIS DOMINA:

205   Quicquid vestra probitas firmat et auctoritas
nuntietur alias per omnes ecclesias;
nostrisque sororibus, puellis claustralibus,
faciamus cognitum quid sit eis vetitum.
Omnia quae diximus quaeque confirmavimus
210   non ullo sophismate sint sub anathemate,
sed rationabiliter fiat et perenniter,
nisi sic paeniteant, clericis ut faveant.
Huius banni ratio vestro sit consilio.
Igitur attendite, "Amen" tantum dicite.

EXCOMMUNICATIO REBELLARUM:

215   Vobis, iussu Veneris, et ubique ceteris
quae vos militaribus subditis amoribus,
maneat confusio, terror et contritio,
labor, infelicitas, dolor et anxietas,
timor et tristitia, bellum et discordia,
220   faex insipientiae, cultus inconstantiae,
dedecus et taedium, longum et opprobrium,
Furiarum species, luctus et pernicies.

  Luna, Iovis famula, Phoebus, suus vernula,
  propter ista crimina negent vobis lumina.
225 Sic sine solamine careatis lumine.
  Nulla dies celebris trahat vos de tenebris.
  Ira Iovis caelitus destruat vos penitus.
  Huius mundi gaudia vobis sint opprobria.
  Omnibus horribiles et abominabiles
230 semper sitis clericis, quae favetis laicis.
  Nemo vobis etiam "Ave" dicat obviam.
  Vestra quoque gaudia sint sine concordia.
  Vobis sit intrinsecus dolor et extrinsecus.
  Vivatis cotidie in lacu miseriae.
235 Pudor, ignominia vobis sint per omnia.
  Laboris et taedii vel pudoris nimii
  sed si quid residuum, sit vobis perpetuum
  nisi, spretis laicis, faveatis clericis.
  Si qua paenituerit atque satisfecerit,
240 dando paenitentiam consequetur veniam.

<OMNES:>

  Ad confirmationem omnes dicimus Amen.

MILITIBUS VICTIS, CESSIT VICTORIA CLERO.

Commentary

Abbreviations

CL: Classical Latin
ML: Medieval Latin
R: manuscript from Rommersdorf, now in Koblenz (Landeshauptarchiv 162, 1401), mid-twelfth century. See **Introduction**, p. 3.
T: manuscript in Trier (Stadtbibliothek 1081), thirteenth century. See **Introduction**, p. 3.

1-24: The nuns of Remiremont hold a unique Council on the subject of Love.

1. **Veris:** < *ver, veris*: "spring."
   sub: with words of time, either "just before" or "just after."
2. **Romarici montium:** Remiremont; see Introduction, p. 1.
3. **contio:** = *conventio*; in CL, typically a political assembly. Here the subject of *habuit.*
   coenobio: < *coenobium*, from two Greek words meaning "shared" and "life"; hence "a commune, monastery, convent."
4. **Tale:** Forms of this word occur often in the *Concilium Romarici Montis*. It is characteristic in ML of formal and technical language, especially that of law and philosophy; consequently elsewhere it tends to lend an air of pretentiousness.
6. **sed neque:** This somewhat redundant combination (= simply *neque*) is a favorite of the poet; it occurs again in ll. 65, 80, and 166 (in this last instance, the *neque* is omitted in R).
7. **negotio:** here the equivalent of "agenda" or "subject."
8. **Amoris:** See **Introduction**, p. 3 and footnote 4.
   tractatum est: < *tracto*, "handle," frequentative of *traho*, "pull." Impersonal verb; translate "there was discussion."
   nullo: sc. *alio concilio.*
9. **Evangelio:** < *Evangelium*, "the Gospel"; from a Greek word meaning literally "good news."

11. **de longe:** "from afar." The preposition *de* in ML develops a great many new uses, which parallel developments in the Romance languages.
12. **laici:** "laymen" (= nonmembers of the clergy). From a Greek word meaning "the people."
13. **Tullensibus:** the people (here men; see *quorum* in following line) of Toul, a town about 55 miles from Remiremont.
14. **quorum:** clearly so in both T and R; Meyer queries the possibility of emending to *quarum*, which makes sense, but would change the scenario drastically and unnecessarily. Retaining the reading of the manuscripts suggests that the *Tullenses* here are the same as the *laici* of the preceding stanza.

    solacium: a common euphemism in ML love poetry that refers to pleasure rather than more narrowly to solace; see ll. 69, 92, 187, 190.
15. I have moved this line here from its position in TR after l. 12. Other editors are satisfied to leave it where it is, although it then refers back to the preceding stanza and not to what follows in this one, contrary to the usage elsewhere in the poem.

    intus et: = *et intus*. The author of the *Concilium Romarici Montis* favors postponing conjunctions and other introductory words within their clauses. The matter is obscured by variant readings of the manuscripts in several of the possible instances. Still there remain enough clear cases to justify calling attention to the phenomenon; the textual vacilation can be explained as scribal attempts to avoid what was felt as awkwardness. See below, with notes on the problematical cases, ll. 32 (in R only), 33 (in T only), 47 (probably, but only by emendation), 51, 87 (twice, the second instance in T only), 212, and 237 (where there is a variant reading in both T and R).
16. For the assumption of a lacuna here, see **Introduction**, p. 5.
19. **custodia:** The abstract noun here by metonymy = *custos*; or perhaps the author regards it as the feminine agent noun.

    haec: hardly a true demonstrative; it adds the sense of "familiar" or "well known."
20. **miles:** an ironic word in the context of this poem.
21. In R, the two halves of this line appear in reverse order.

    invita: < *invitus*, "unwilling, reluctant."
22. **Veteranae:** a term with military associations (like its English derivative); See on l. 20 above.

arcentur: < *arceo*, "bar, turn away."
23. taedium: "annoyance, disgust"; a somewhat stronger word than the English derivative, "tedium."

25-48: The opening ceremonies of the Council are described.

27. This and the following line are omitted in R.
28. Lectrix: In T, the only witness to the text here, this word is garbled, but enough is legible to support this emendation by Waitz.
29. Danubrio: Danubrium was a medieval market village near Remiremont; it survives today only in the personal name Deneuvre.
    officio: From its literal meaning in CL, "duty," this word comes to refer in ML to a prayer or church service. "Office," in this sense, will do as a translation, or "service, ceremony, performance."
30. artis amatoriae: the name of Ovid's work referred to in l. 27. It occurs again just below, in l. 35.
31. Cantus: genitive singular, with *modulamina*, "measures."
32. satis et: See note on *intus et*, l. 32. R here reads *satisque*.
33. non quaelibet: "not just anyone."
    duae sed: See note on *intus et*, l. 15. R here reads *Eva et*.
34. latuit: < *lateo*, "be hidden from, be a secret from"; with accusative. Its subject here is *quicquid Amor statuit*.
36. opere: "from experience," the equivalent of the Greek *praxis*; contrasts with *notitia* in the previous line which is to be understood as "theoretical knowledge."
    facere: object of *sciat*; "what a man knows (how) to do."
37. oblectamina: "delights" < *oblectamen* < *oblecto*.
38. adstitit: < *adsto*, "stand up."
    indicto: < *indico*, "call for, demand."
39. qua refloruit: "in which she was like a flower." In l. 43 she is explicitly identified with a flower.
41. gemmis . . . auro: ablatives of comparison.
44. For the placement of this line, see **Introduction**, p. 5.
46. talis: sc., as the poet has described her.
47. habens et: See note on *intus et*, l. 15. Both T and R lack *et* here, but a syllable is needed to complete the rhythm.
    secundum: functions as a preposition; "according to, proportional to, in keeping with." She is as eloquent as if she had studied rhetoric.
48. coetus: "assembly, meeting."

ora sic aperuit: Biblical language (Job 33.2, Ecclesiasticus 51.33, etc.) made additionally high-flown here by the use of the plural *ora*.

49-60: The *Cardinalis Domina* declares that she has been sent to inquire into the ways of the women of Remiremont.

49. lascivia: does not have the derogatory connotation of the English derivative, but a proper English translation is hard to find. Something like "sportiveness, fun-loving quality, frolicsomeness" will have to do. The word occurs again in l. 113.
50. Aprilis cum Maio: = *Aprilis et Maii*, used for the sake of the rhyme.
51. facimus: The *Cardinalis Domina* here refers to herself with the majestic or royal "we." She is subsequently inconsistent in this regard, shifting between singular and plural.
    ad vos quare: See note on *intus et*, l. 15.
    venimus: Typically indirect questions have their verb in the subjunctive in CL. Exceptions, as here, are common in colloquial usage; e.g., comedy.
52. quotquot: "however many"; indeclinable. Also in l. 138.
53. visere: The infinitive expressing purpose as a substitute for *ut* with the subjunctive (or a gerund or gerundive construction) is uncommon in CL until the later period.
56. obtestor: "implore."
57. vestrum: not the possessive adjective, but the genitive of the pronoun *vos* in a partitive sense, here with *nulla*: "let no one of you . . . "
    quae vos vita teneat: The whole phrase functions as the object of *sileat* < *sileo*, "keep silent about, suppress, fail to reveal."
58. For the assumption of a lacuna here, see **Introduction**, p. 5.
59. si cui parcendum est: impersonal passive of an intransitive verb: "if anyone is to be shown mercy."
60. meum est: "it is up to me, my prerogative."

61-108: Several of the women speak of their devotion to the service of love, exclusively the love of clerks rather than of knights.

61. ex quo: sc. *tempore*; "from the time when, ever since."
63. inscienter: adverb based on *scio*; "unwittingly."
64. servando: The ablative of the gerund and a simple participle are often logically interchangeable: "we, by holding to our

rule" = "we, holding to our rule." Similarly in l. 240. In ML the use of the gerund sometimes extends even to cases where it is strictly illogical; e.g., in l. 150. The instance in l. 99 comes after a lacuna, making it impossible to determine to which class it belongs. See also note on l. 168.

65. **habendam:** sc. *esse*, indirect statement with *eligimus*. The subject of the indirect discourse is *copulam*. "We choose not to have an association with any man." *Copulam* is also understood as the object of *cognovimus*, and it governs *talis hominis*.

    sed neque: See note on l. 6.
67. This and the following two lines are omitted in R.
69. **nil tardat:** *Nil* is the inner object of *tardat*, and *solacia* is its regular (outer) object. Translate: "makes no delaying of pleasures."
72. **quos:** antecedent is *clericorum*.

    scimus affabiles: sc. *esse*.
73. **curialitas:** < *curialis* < *curia*, "court, senate house." *Curialitas*, not a CL word, may be translated "courtesy," but in the special medieval, not in the modern sense; "courtliness" is perhaps preferable.

    clericis: dative governed by prefix of compound verb.
74. **fallere:** The infinitive in ML comes to function much more readily than in CL as a noun, so that *posse*, for example, commonly means "power." Here translate, "They do not know how to deceive."
75. **peritiam:** = skill and experience combined.
76. **foedera:** usually a military or political term; here pacts of love.
77. **quid:** for *aliquid*, after *si*. To account for the neuter, this may be construed as an inner object. An accurate (if somewhat inelegant) translation then would be, "If they do any loving . . . " For this syntax, compare l. 105.
78. **assumpsimus:** < *ad* + *sumo*, "single out, choose."
80. **sed neque:** See note on l. 6.
82. **Experto:** < *experior*. The participle is used in both the active and the passive sense: either "one who has experienced, an expert," or "a thing that has been experienced, evidence." The gender here calls for the latter interpretation, while the relative pronoun *cui* seems to call for the former. The general sense is clear enough, and perhaps we must let it go at that.
84. **labilis:** < *labor, labi*, "slippery, fickle."
85. **insipientiam:** the opposite of *sapientia*.

notitiam: "acquaintance."
87. **dolus ut:** See note on *intus et*, l. 15. The reading of T, *in eis qui*, farther on in this line is another instance of the same pattern; R reads *qui in eis*.
in eis: As here printed (see preceding note) this could be taken equally with the phrase before it or after it; it is very likely intended to be felt with both.
88. **nos:** accusative.
notavimus: < *noto*, "indicate, mention."
89. **dilectio:** "love, esteem."
vitio: "blemish, sin."
91. **ulterius:** "hereafter."
92. **valet:** "is able"; introduced by *quod* in the previous line. Main verb in a clause of indirect discourse, frequently so expressed in ML rather than with an infinitive as in CL. Governs *disiungere* in the following line.
94. **claustralibus:** "cloistered" < *claustrum*, "enclosure," < *claudo*.
95. **susceptio:** "acceptance."
97. For the assumption of a lacuna here, see **Introduction**, p. 5.
99. **amplectendo:** See note on l. 64.
recuso: "reject."
103. **Tali:** such as has just been described.
105. **quid:** for *aliquid*, after *si*; inner object of normally intransitive *peccavimus*. "If we have sinned any (sin)."
107. **adeo:** "to the same extent." With *quam*, "as," in the following line. Both T and R here read *audio*.
108. **laudibus:** can be taken with *in omnibus*: "in all your praises," or as an instrumental ablative, in which case *in omnibus* means, "in all respects."

109-132: Those who favor the knights now speak in their turn.

110. **Amoris:** See **Introduction**, p. 3 and footnote 4.
112. **nobis sunt memoriae:** "are in our thoughts"; a double dative.
113. **lascivia:** See note on l. 49.
114. **obsequium:** "compliance with, being agreeable to."
115. **pro nostra gratia:** "to win our favor."
118. **praeelegimus:** < *prae + e + lego*, "give preference to."
121. **sectam:** in CL usually refers to a philosophical "school" rather than what we mean by its derivative, "sect." Here perhaps may be translated, "class of men."
122. **habere:** Whatever is to be understood as the direct object of this verb is left vague.

124. This and the following two lines are omitted in R.
   magis: sc. *placet.*
   psalterium: "a psalter (copy of the Book of Psalms)."
125. **legere:** sc. *psalterium.*
126. **parvi pendo:** "I little value." *Parvi* is genitive of value.
   regulam: the Rule by which her religious order was formally governed.
127. **pervium:** "accessible, open."
128. **congrua:** "suitable."
129. **exposuimus:** "opened to, placed at the disposal of, made available to." Parking problems are not an altogether recent phenomenon.
   novimus: sc. *esse.*
130. **summopere:** adverb, "very greatly, exceedingly" = *summo opere. Magnopere* and *tantopere* also occur.
131. R omits from here through line 162. Since T does not generally indicate changes of speaker, in this passage they must be inferred by the editor.

133-153: A representative of the faction of the clerks speaks in their favor once more.

133. **parum:** "too little"
   regnavimus: somewhat obscure; perhaps, "we have been our own mistresses." The general sense of the line is clear enough: the speakers are still young and inexperienced.
135. **clero:** "the clergy, clerks."
137. **ad libitum:** "at our pleasure, as it pleases us"; or it may be, "at their pleasure." Most likely the author intends a little of both.
138. This entire line is in apposition with *debitum* above.
   viro: T, the only witness for the text here, reads *virgo.* Emendation seems to be called for, although a forced case could be made for the manuscript reading.
141. **nos:** accusative.
   mutabimus: "exchange, give up, renounce."
143. **quaerit studium:** The phrase is probably chosen for the sake of the rhyme, and does not really yield much sense. Perhaps "seeks excuses," or "demands enthusiasm."
   ridet: "smiles at." *Gaudia* is the direct object. The ladies cite no evidence to support their proposition.
145. **rhythmis atque versibus:** Greek and Latin words for more or less the same thing: poems.

147. This line is garbled in T, the only witness for the text at this point; it reads: *Dulcis amicia clericis est et gloria*. In the margin appear the cryptic letters *Dane*, and there is extra space left after the line. The emendations adopted here make sense of the line, including metrically, but there can be no certainty. The puzzle of *Dane* remains.
148. **aliae ... opere:** so in both T and R, producing an intolerably poor rhyme; the first half of this line is identical with that of line 140, where the rhyme is correct. Should we here read *alterae* (that is, *altere*)? See **Introduction**, footnote 5.
149. **habilis:** "capable, competent, adept."
150. **habendo:** See note on l. 64.
152. **habeatur irritum:** "let it be regarded as null and void."
153. **absque:** "free of"; preposition with ablative.

154-171: The *Cardinalis Domina* calls for the Council's verdict. They pronounce emphatically on the side of the clerks.

156. **quarum:** subjective genitives.
157. **gratia:** "favor, good will."
158. **quibus:** antecedent is *militum*, although a case could be made for *notitia et ... gratia*.
159. **detegere:** < *de* + *tego*, "uncover, reveal."
161. **odibiles:** "hateful" < *odi*. Here feminine.
164. It seems probable that the lacuna at this point includes a change of speaker; there may be other unmarked changes of speaker in this passage as well.
166. **sed neque:** See note on l. 6. R here omits *neque*.
168. *vitando ducimus* T; *vitando dicimus* R. Emendation seems called for, although some sort of sense can be wrested out of the readings of either manuscript, perhaps by the application of the procedure noted on l. 64. As here emended, with *vitandos* understand *esse*, and *ducimus* has the sense of "we consider, regard as."
169. **sapere:** parallel with *bonum*.

172-204: The *Cardinalis Domina* accepts the verdict, and declares that violators are to be shunned.

172. **iure consulitis:** "duly give as your advice."
173. **eas:** that is, those who favor knights.
    consortio: "companionship."

175. **paenituerint:** This verb does not occur with a personal subject in standard CL; but see ll. 212 and 239 below. This is the reading of T. R has *respuerint*, which is unmetrical, but may easily be emended to *resipuerint* < *re* + *sapio*, "come to one's senses," the opposite of *desipere* (see l. 195). The reading of R, with this emendation, may well be preferable.
176. **talis:** "the following."
177. **ne sic peccent amplius:** This clause defines the *condicio* of the previous line as an indirect command: "the following condition, that they should . . . "
178. **Hoc . . . obedientiam:** "We charge you to obey the following as well."
180. **Uni soli:** dative singular (all genders).
181. **banno:** This is the only word without classical roots in the entire poem (unless we wish also to count *amen*, ll. 214 and 241). The Germanic *bann* was a public proclamation, often, as here, a denunciation. It survives in English "ban" and "banish," and it is still familiar in the archaic phrase, "posting the banns," publicly announcing a forthcoming marriage.
184. **sed non sub silentio:** "not bound by a rule of silence."
185. **vos:** nominative; an emphatic subject. The object of *detis* is *tactum* in the next line.
   vilibus: < *vilis*, "lowborn." A separate group from the *militibus* farther on in the line.
186. **vel coxae vel femoris:** It is a little puzzling why the *Cardinalis Domina* should here be so explicit anatomically. The reading of the rather inappropriate *coxae* ("hip") is not perfectly clear in T; *colli* and *cordis* have been suggested as emendations. *Femoris* may be chosen simply for the sake of the rhyme.
189. For the assumption of a lacuna here, see **Introduction**, p. 5.
191. **cum non creditur:** "(even) when one does not expect it."
192. **quorum:** antecedent is *militum* in l. 190.
194. **sapientia:** ablative.
195. **totum quicquid:** "absolutely everything."
   desipimus: < *de* + *sapio*, "relax, seek pleasure."
196. **Causas...regere:** "to act on our behalf and manage our affairs." *Causas nostras agere* in CL would mean "to plead our cases"; but *causa* has here acquired its ML sense as virtually the equivalent of *res* (reflected in modern French *chose* and Spanish and Italian *cosa*).
198. **abdita:** < *abdo, -ere* < *ab* + *do, dare*, "secrets."

201. **haec:** subject (feminine singular). The line is garbled in R: *Et si cui his placeat hos neque taceat.*

205-241: The *Cardinalis Domina* pronounces an awful curse on all who fail to conform to the new orthodoxy.

206. **alias:** could be construed with *ecclesias*, but is most likely to be taken as the adverb, "elsewhere."
208. **vetitum:** T here reads *vitium*.
210. T for this line has only *Non ullo sophismate* and then breaks off. R reads *Cum nostro sophismate sint sub anathemate*. The line may plausibly be reconstructed as here by combining the two sources.
    sophismate: ablative case of *sophisma*, a Greek word; best taken as truncated ablative absolute ("there being no . . ."). If the reading suggested in the preceding note is adopted, *sophisma* would have its common meaning of "subterfuge, specious reasoning"; freely, "mincing words." If the reading of R is accepted, then it has its literal meaning, "wisdom."
    anathemate: < *anathema* (Greek), "curse."
211. **rationabiliter:** The line as it is in T is metrically faulty. R reads *rationabile*, which scans and can be made to yield a kind of sense, but does not rhyme. Probably the *-tio-* is to be pronounced as one syllable,
212. **paeniteant:** See note on 1.175.
    clericis ut: See note on *intus et*, l. 15.
213. **Huius . . . consilio:** = let this ban be ratified by your wisdom
215 (Subhead). **REBELLARUM:** Since *rebellis* belongs to the third declension, this form is an outright solecism. (Only in T; R reads simply EXCOMMUNICATIO.)
215. **Vobis:** like *ceteris* at the end of the line, dative of disadvantage with *maneat* in l. 217.
216. **subditis:** < *sub + do*, "subject (oneself)." Present indicative.
217. The curse that runs breathlessly from here almost to the end of the poem is like an operatic patter song. Some of it seems to be mere sound and fury (for example, what is the meaning of *cultus inconstantiae* in l. 220?) but it is all amusing.
220. **faex:** "dregs."
222. **species:** "appearance."

223. **famula ... vernula:** Both mean "servant." *Vernula* (masculine of the first declension) refers to Phoebus, the sun, and *suus* refers back to *Iovis*.
226. **dies celebris:** "special day."
227. **caelitus:** adverb, "from heaven."
    penitus: adverb, "utterly."
231. **obviam:** "when they encounter you."
236. **Laboris ... taedii ... pudoris:** These genitives are all partitive with *si quid*: "But if anything remains (if I have omitted anything) of hardship," etc.
237. **si quid:** For the position of these words relative to the partitive genitives they govern, see note on *intus et*, l. 15. T here reads: *si quid residuum* (without *sed*), and R reads unmetrically *sed si quid est residuum*.
238. **spretis:** < *sperno*, "spurn, disdain."
239. **paenituerit:** see note on l. 175.
241. For the two lines that conclude the poem, see above, Introduction, p. 4.